DO-IT-YOURSELF
BRAIN
SURGERY

DO-IT-YOURSELF BRAIN SURGERY

and Other Implausibly Titled Books

With an Introduction by JOEL RICKETT

BLOOMSBURY

NEW YORK · BERLIN · LONDON

Published by Bloomsbury USA, New York

All papers used by Bloomsbury USA are natural, recyclable products made from wood grown in well-managed forests. The manufacturing processes conform to the environmental regulations of the country of origin.

Library of Congress Control Number: 2009925534

ISBN-13 978-1-60819-019-5

Published in the United Kingdom in 2008 by Aurum Press under the title
How to Avoid Huge Ships
First U.S. Edition 2009

1 3 5 7 9 10 8 6 4 2

Printed by 1010 Printing International Ltd

INTRODUCTION

'Glory be to God for dappled things …
All things counter, original, spare, strange.'
Gerard Manley Hopkins, 'Pied Beauty' (1918)

WHAT MAKES A BOOK TITLE TRULY ODD? I don't mean merely quaint, funny or outlandish; I mean utterly, remarkably, jaw-droppingly bizarre. Scientists have toiled for years researching this question; perhaps the answer will always remain elusive. Yet we instantly recognize oddness when we see it. For example, take a book such as *Bombproof Your Horse*. If the authors had opted for an alternative equestrian title (*Train Your Horse*, say) their work would never have raised eyebrows.

After wading through thousands of odd book titles for this seminal collection, I believe that a degree of ignorance is essential. The writers and publishers must be oblivious to the sheer queerness of their choice, usually because they are so close to the subject that they cannot see its absurdity. Take the photographer who lovingly documented the strange skin decorations and ornaments he found in a far-flung land. He believed there was only one choice when titling the resulting book: *Tattooed Mountain Women and Spoon Boxes of Daghestan*. Or recall the British Crop Protection Council researcher who believed his study needed a visionary title, opting for *Weeds in a Changing World*. Often writers miss the potential double meaning of their masterpiece. When the European Commission's top physicists were compiling recent developments in steel research, they had no qualms about calling the resulting book *The Physical Properties of Slags*.

For thirty years the oddest of these odd titles have been found and celebrated by the *Bookseller* magazine's Diagram Prize for Oddest Book Title of the Year. Forget the Booker, the Nobel or the Pulitzer: real book lovers and the literati agree that the Diagram transcends them all. Every year entries flood in from around the world, starting a spell of frenzied voting and blanket media coverage.

This hunt for 'unlikely' book titles was originally suggested by publisher Bruce Robertson as a diversion for bored visitors to the Frankfurt Book Fair. For the uninitiated, Frankfurt is a kind of global clearing house for books, a soulless collection of giant sheds with hundreds of thousands of titles on display. Robertson hoped his wheeze would provide publishers with a moment's diversion while plodding the aisles, a way to avoid those chain-smoking continental editors and cigar-chomping Americans. His idea was simple but effective. Many of the earliest discoveries were by no means vintage – the best were *100 Years of British Rail Catering*, *Cooking with God*, and *50 New Poodle Grooming Styles*. But there was a single standout title: *Proceedings of the Second International Workshop on Nude Mice*, published by the University of Tokyo Press. The Diagram Prize was born.

The Frankfurt Book Fair has been running since the twelfth century. It is intriguing to imagine what would have been discovered by, say, Martin Luther, if he had been scouring the stands for odd titles. Certainly we know that spotters in the nineteenth century would have been spoilt for choice; the Victorians blended objective enquiry with a gruesome oddness. Three classics that immediately come to mind are *Dentologia: A Poem on the Diseases of the Teeth*, *Premature Burial and How It May Be Prevented*, and *The Romance of Leprosy*.

From the early days the procedures of the Diagram Prize appear to have been deliberately vague. Run by the *Bookseller* magazine's diarist Horace Bent, a legendary book-trade figure, the winners seem to have been settled by an elite, anonymous group, probably over port at a London club. Any type of book was admissible, with the only restriction being that publishers were not allowed to submit their own books, to screen out intentional efforts at oddness. In 1993 submissions were opened beyond the confines of Frankfurt: immediately readers of the *Bookseller* (bookshop staff, academics, editors, librarians and literary agents) started scanning through the endless lists of new titles. As publishing output spiralled, there were rich pickings. And when the major publishing corporations tried to squeeze any remaining oddness out of the industry, digital printing technology sprung up, enabling quirkier small publishers to produce books for niche interests (no matter how specific). The Diagram judges resisted the temptation to allow books from vanity presses – it would be too easy for people to invent odd titles just to win the prize. All shortlisted books must be properly published, in a bid to reach a defined – if elusive – audience.

Merrily scanning the lists of Diagram Prize winners and runners-up, it is clear that the gloriously sincere endeavours of medical research have provided one of the richest seams over the thirty years. Just imagine leafing through some of these suggestively titled works: *A Pictorial Book of Tongue*

Coatings, *A Colour Atlas of Posterior Chamber Implants*, or *Inflammatory Bowel Diseases: A Personal View*. Being so obsessed with their narrow field of research, medical authors often seem to miss ambiguity. So *Practical Infectious Diseases* was presumably not a how-to guide to infecting your enemies, while the 2003 favourite *Hot Topics in Urology* sounds painfully relevant.

Nature's glories have often been celebrated in book form. I imagine that there was an avid, if specialist, readership for *Six-Legged Sex: The Erotic Lives of Bugs*, as well as *Neurosis Induced Cannibalism in Antarctic Pigs* (brilliantly edited by Pigman Press). Farmers everywhere presumably flocked to bookshops to snap up a copy of *The Potatoes of Bolivia: Their Breeding, Value and Evolutionary Relationships*. That's if the Celtic ones weren't already busy reading (and perhaps road-testing) the very personal manual titled *Sex Instructions for Irish Farmers*.

Every respectable household still has its fair share of 'how-to' and hobby books; perhaps your own shelves include *Drying Flowers With a Microwave*, or *Waterproofing Your Child*. You are less likely to have a copy of the rare 1989 Diagram winner, *How to Shit in the Woods*, which was aimed at people who needed an entire book to learn this 'lost art'. And what gentleman could live without the *Braces Owners Manual: A Guide to the Wearing and Care of Braces*, or the essential companion to facial hygiene that is *Nasal Maintenance*? To our enlightened ears, some of the books published in an earlier age can sound morally dubious. But we must be careful not to judge the men who, in the early 1980s, followed the advice set out in *Wife Battering: A Systems Theory Approach*. Perhaps their spouses took revenge by learning from the classic *Interpersonal Violence: The Practical Series.*

As with any high-profile literary award, controversies have rocked the Diagram over the years. There were several dark stretches where no prize was awarded at all (who could imagine the Booker Prize admitting that no novel was worthy of the accolade?). When public voting was introduced in 2000 – via the newfangled interweb – the prize's custodian Horace Bent threatened to resign. How could his impeccable judgement be disregarded in favour of the teeming multitudes? However, despite his outburst reaching the diary columns of the national newspapers, Mr Bent failed to carry out his promise, and eventually contented himself with drawing up the short list and giving most publicity to his favoured titles. I refuse to believe the rumours of bribery and rigged polling.

The Diagram is unique, and perhaps uniquely blessed, in that spotters and judges alike do not actually have to read the books in question. Indeed they are actively discouraged from doing so, in case a close knowledge of the subject makes them realize the book is less odd than it first appears. The imagination should be allowed to run wild, particularly with those books which seem preoccupied with blindingly obvious topics. Why, we wonder, did the author need so many pages to explain the art of *Big and Very Big Hole Drilling*? And why did the writer believe people required an entire book on his *Method For Calculating the Size of Stone Needed for Closing End-Tipped Rubble Banks in Rivers*? Did the level of local interest really merit an entire tome about the question *Did Lewis Carroll Visit Llandudno?* Surely a simple yes or no would have sufficed.

Sometimes this habit of using an entire book to tackle a single issue seems positively reckless. When the captain of your little pleasure cruiser spots a ferry hull looming over the horizon, do you really want him to reach for a copy of *How to Avoid Huge Ships*? Or would you rather that he kept his attentions on the wheel?

It is inevitable that some of the oddest winning titles appeal to our basest emotions, but new depths have been plumbed in the last decade. The first suggestive title was *Archaeology in the American Bottom* in 1993 (was that book about real excavations in the posteriors of American citizens, or is bottom archaeology an American skill to be explained and exported?). In 1997 came the highly creative *The Joy of Sex: Pocket Edition*. But in 2000 the vulgarities of public voting ushered in the most debased winner yet: an engineering manual called *High Performance Stiffened Structures*. It is also worth noting a repeated fascination with lesbianism, which some readers clearly still find adds an extra level of oddity. So we have 1990's *Lesbian Sadomasochism Safety Manual*, as well as the 2003 champion, *The Big Book of Lesbian Horse Stories*.

Winning the Diagram brings no immediate monetary reward for the author; instead it is the spotter of the title who receives a bottle of the 'fairly passable' (usually claret). But most winning authors have been delighted at the accolade and the ensuing media attention. From the *Sun* to the *Ohio Journal*, from Russian state media to the BBC World Service, the prize is obsessively reported (and journalists have tried flattery and subterfuge in failed bids to discover the name of the winner before the official announcement). Such publicity can transform the profile of a title, lifting it from academic obscurity to the front of bookshops. The 2006 winner, *The Stray Shopping Carts of Eastern North America: A Guide to Field Identification*, was displayed in stores across the world, its grateful author inundated with offers of interviews. Such coverage has drawn the attention of major corporations, keen to sponsor the award and boost their public image. But unlike the Booker and the Orange Prize, the Diagram has refused all such blandishments: it must retain a higher purity of purpose, unsullied by commercial concerns.

While publishers are not allowed to enter their own titles, the match of title and publishing house is often intriguing. Why did the University of Chicago Press take such interest in releasing a work of trans-European history called *Versailles: The View from Sweden*? Others are more apt: Transaction Press published the essential guidebook *The Madam as Entrepreneur: Career Management in House Prostitution*, while the British Cement Association surely had a vested interest in releasing *Highlights in the History of Concrete* and their other classic, *Lakeside Car Parks*. And when he had completed a reference volume about *Greek Rural Postmen and Their Cancellation Numbers*, who else could the author send his manuscript to but the Hellenic Philatelic Society?

The Diagram Prize's reach is not all-encompassing; some gems take years to come to light. For instance, in 1988 the prize overlooked a classic: *The Gut Contents of Six Leathery Turtles*. But I have subsequently discovered that the world of turtle research is a fertile source of odd titles. There's the useful *Plastic Bags in the Intestinal Tracts of Leatherback Marine Turtles*, or the improbable-sounding *Transatlantic*

Travel by Juvenile Loggerhead Turtle. There's also a turtle-related tract called *Rips, Fads, and Little Loggerheads.*

Sometimes odd titles can uncover whole new worlds. Take *Proceedings of the 18th International Seaweed Symposium.* Who would have known that since 1973, scientists have been meeting regularly to discuss pressing developments in seaweed (the next Seaweed Symposium is scheduled for Mexico 2010). I wonder if the same commitment has been shown in other fields. Did *Proceedings of the Sixth International Fatigue Congress* have any sequels, or did the participants all grow tired of the ritual?

It's all too easy to sneer at some of these books. But oddness is in the eye of the beholder. Thanks to amazon.com we discover that some readers loved *The Stray Shopping Carts of Eastern North America*: a certain S. Fragomen hails it as a 'hilariously depressing work', while A.J. Fries observes that 'the author's language coupled with his beautiful photography give the lowly carts individual personalities'. And while *People Who Don't Know They're Dead* picked up some terrible reviews, the book helped Mr Jeffrey Duncan: 'It sheds light on an area of the paranormal not often discussed, the idea of hitchhiker spirits ... I felt as if I personally knew the folks being written about. There is much wisdom here.'

Long live odd titles, and long live the *Bookseller*'s Diagram Prize. If you ever spot a contender, send a note to bent@bookseller.co.uk. Fame and fortune awaits.

JOEL RICKETT

DEPUTY EDITOR, THE BOOKSELLER

ACKNOWLEDGEMENTS

'I've made an odd discovery…'
Bertrand Russell

Thanks to Bruce Robertson of the Diagram Group, who started it all (and who continues to be a champion spotter). Thanks to Aurum Press, who had the wonderfully odd idea for this book of odd books. Thanks to all the staff of the *Bookseller* who have been involved in the prize over the last thirty years, particularly former editors Louis Baum and Nicholas Clee, current editor-in-chief Neill Denny, and the magazine's former information manager Colin Randall, whose diligent archiving made this book so simple to create.

But the biggest thanks are saved for the *Bookseller* readers who have suggested hundreds of odd titles and voted for their favourites. Those who spotted Diagram Prize winners were: Elfreda Powell, David Martin, Colin Eccleshare, Russell Ash, Sally Whitaker, Trevor Bounford, Mark Bryant, Desmond Elliott, Shad Helmstetter, Anne Tannahill, John Doyle, Stuart Booth, David Harris, Brian Shawcross, Simon Tuite, Nach Waxman, Nicholas Essen, Kate Santon, E.P. Kelly, M.J. Grant, Judith Seaman, Clare Gilliam, David Pearson, Mark Campbell, Neal Maillet, Jon Howells, David Evans, Graeme Henderson, and David Leonard.

DESIGN FOR IMPACT
50 Years of Airline Safety Cards

Eric Ericson & Johan Pihl

Princeton Architectural Press, 2003

Illustrated coffee-table book about airline
safety cards.

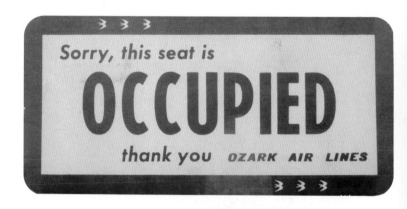

DESIGN FOR IMPACT

FIFTY YEARS OF AIRLINE SAFETY CARDS

www.papress.com

REMOVE FROM BOOKSHELF

OLD TRACTORS
and the Men Who Love Them

Roger Welsch

MBI Publishing Company, 1995

Memoir of author's love affair with tractors.

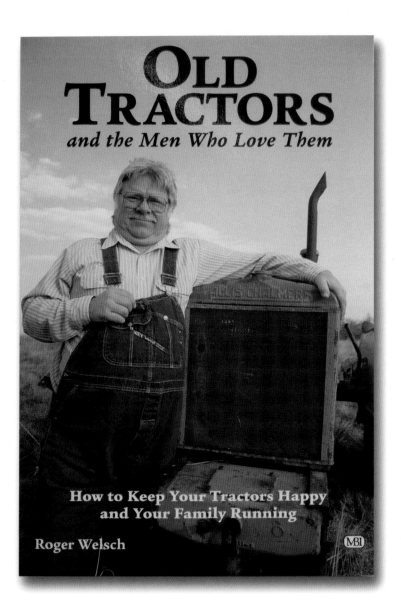

HOW TO AVOID HUGE SHIPS

Captain John W. Trimmer

self-published, 1982

How to keep out of harm's way at sea.

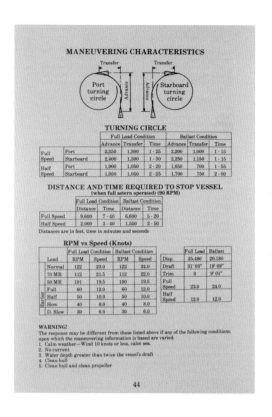

MANEUVERING CHARACTERISTICS

Transfer   Transfer

Port turning circle   Advance   Advance   Starboard turning circle

TURNING CIRCLE

		Full Load Condition			Ballast Condition		
		Advance	Transfer	Time	Advance	Transfer	Time
Full Speed	Port	2,350	1,300	1 - 25	2,290	1,000	1 - 15
	Starboard	2,400	1,300	1 - 30	2,250	1,150	1 - 15
Half Speed	Port	1,900	1,050	2 - 20	1,650	790	1 - 55
	Starboard	1,950	1,050	2 - 25	1,700	750	2 - 00

DISTANCE AND TIME REQUIRED TO STOP VESSEL
(when full astern operated) (90 RPM)

	Full Load Condition		Ballast Condition	
	Distance	Time	Distance	Time
Full Speed	9,600	7 - 40	6,600	5 - 20
Half Speed	2,000	3 - 40	1,550	2 - 50

Distances are in feet, time in minutes and seconds

RPM vs Speed (Knots)

		Full Load Condition		Ballast Condition				Full Load	Ballast
	Load	RPM	Speed	RPM	Speed		Disp.	35,480	29,180
	Normal	122	23.0	122	24.0		Draft	31' 03"	19' 09"
	70 MR	112	21.5	112	22.0		Trim	0	9' 01"
	50 MR	101	19.5	100	19.5		Full Speed	23.0	24.0
Harbor	Full	60	12.0	60	12.0				
	Half	50	10.0	50	10.0		Half Speed	12.0	12.0
	Slow	40	8.0	40	8.0				
	D. Slow	30	6.0	30	6.0				

WARNING!
The response may be different from those listed above if any of the following conditions, upon which the maneuvering information is based are varied.
1. Calm weather—Wind 10 knots or less, calm sea.
2. No current
3. Water depth greater than twice the vessel's draft
4. Clean hull
5. Clean hull and clean propeller

44

HOW TO AVOID HUGE SHIPS
OR
I NEVER MET A SHIP I LIKED

by
CAPTAIN JOHN W. TRIMMER

Master Mariner & Deep Sea Towing Master
Licensed Panama Canal Pilot
Active Washington State Pilot

NOT A COURSE IN THE RULES OF THE ROAD

NUCLEAR WAR: What's In It For You?

Ground Zero War Foundation

Methuen, 1982

Everything you ever wanted to know about nuclear war.

Why do you feel scared with 10,000 nuclear weapons protecting you?

NUCLEAR WAR

What's in it for you?

GROUND ZERO

methuen

HOW GREEN WERE THE NAZIS?

Franz-Josef Brüggemeier, Mark Cioc
& Thomas Zeller (editors)

Ohio University Press, 2005

Environmentalism under the Third Reich.

BEYOND LEAF RAKING

Peter L. Benson & Eugene C. Roehlkepartain

Abingdon Press, 1993

How to integrate
service-learning
into youth
ministry.

Edited by Franz-Josef Brüggemeier, Mark Cioc, and Thomas Zeller

How Green Were the Nazis?

*Nature, Environment, and Nation
in the Third Reich*

HIGHLIGHTS IN THE HISTORY OF CONCRETE

Christopher C. Stanley

Cement and Concrete Association, 1979

Noteworthy developments in the history of the building material.

Concrete work in ancient Egypt, c. 1950 BC.

Cement and Concrete Association

Highlights in

The History of Concrete

Christopher C. Stanley

THE STRAY SHOPPING CARTS
OF EASTERN NORTH AMERICA
A Guide to Field Identification

Julian Montague

Abrams Image, 2006

How to identify abandoned shopping trolleys.

THE
STRAY
SHOPPING
CARTS OF EASTERN
NORTH AMERICA

A GUIDE TO FIELD IDENTIFICATION

JULIAN MONTAGUE

WHAT TO SAY WHEN YOU TALK TO YOUR SELF

Shad Helmstetter

Thorsons, 1986

Self-help manual.

WHAT TO SAY WHEN YOU TALK TO YOUR SELF

Powerful *new* techniques to programme your potential for success!

Shad Helmstetter

VERSAILLES
The View from Sweden

Elaine Evans Dee & Guy Walton

Cooper-Hewitt Museum, 1988

Exhibition catalogue.

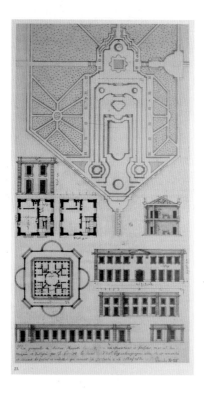

Versailles

The View from Sweden

FABULOUS SMALL JEWS

Joseph Epstein

Houghton Mifflin, 2003

Collection of short stories.

FABULOUS SMALL JEWS

stories by JOSEPH EPSTEIN

GREEK RURAL POSTMEN AND THEIR CANCELLATION NUMBERS

Derek Willan (editor)

Hellenic Philatelic Society of Great Britain, 1994

An exhaustive record of the rural postal routes of Greece.

HELLENIC PHILATELIC SOCIETY OF GREAT BRITAIN

Publication Number 4

GREEK RURAL POSTMEN AND THEIR CANCELLATION NUMBERS

Edited by

DEREK   WILLAN

Price £20.

ITALIAN WITHOUT WORDS

Don Cangelosi & Joseph Delli Carpini

Meadowbrook Press, 1989

How to communicate using Italian body language.

Common Expressions

Help me, please!
Aiutami, per favore!
(ay-OO-tah-mee payr fah-VOH-ray)

Now you can communicate in Italian
even if you don't know a single word.

ITALIAN
WITHOUT
WORDS

Don Cangelosi and Joseph Delli Carpini

THE BOOK OF MARMALADE
Its Antecedents, Its History and
Its Role in the World Today

C. Anne Wilson

Pennsylvania Press, 1999

All you could ever wish to know about marmalade.

C. ANNE WILSON

THE BOOK OF
MARMALADE

THE ANGER OF AUBERGINES

Bulbul Sharma

Spinefex Press, 1998

Collection of short stories.

THE JOY OF CHICKEN

Norma Gilbert

Argent Books, 1977

Cookery book.

the anger of aubergines

bulbul sharma

SPINIFEX

ENTERTAINING WITH INSECTS
The Original Guide to Insect Cookery

Ronald L. Taylor & Barbara J. Carter

Salutek, 1992

Cookery book.

Dry Roasted Insects

Spread fresh, frozen, and cleaned insects on paper towels on a cookie sheet. Bake at 200° for 1-2 hours until desired state of dryness is reached. Check state of dryness by attempting to crush insect with a spoon.

Basic Insect Flour

Dry roast insects (see preceding recipe) and blend in electric blender until a delicate flour is produced. The amount of flour resulting from a given quantity of dry roasted insects varies with the insect used. One cup of bees, for example, reduces to a smaller quantity of flour than does 1 cup of mealworms.

Pastry

For an 8-inch pie crust.

1¼ cups flour
¼ cup bee flour (see preceding recipe)
½ teaspoon salt
½ cup shortening
4 tablespoons water

Mix together flours and salt. Cut in shortening with a pastry blender. Sprinkle with water, a tablespoon at a time. Mix wi[th] a fork until flour is moistened. Mold doug[h] into a ball. Place on a lightly floured boar[d]. Flatten and roll out to about ⅛ inch thick. Keep pastry circular and roll it about 1 i[nch] larger than the inverted pie pan. Fold p[astry] in half and transfer to the pie pan. Unfo[ld] and ease pastry loosely into the pan. Be careful not to stretch. Trim pastry wit[h] scissors ½ inch from edge of pan. Fold pastry under edges of pan. Flute the e[dge]. Hook points under pan rim. Fill and [bake] according to recipe being used.

Entertaining
with Insects

Or: The Original Guide To Insect Cookery

Ronald L. Taylor
Barbara J. Carter

Illustrated by
John Gregory Tweed

---

th

d insects
alt
ite pepper
ry, diced
n lemon juice

on butter
oons onion, finely chopped
on parsley

e all of the ingredients in a saucepan
ng to a boil. Cover and simmer for
. Cool and strain through cheesecloth,
ing firmly to express all the juices.
ure. If less than 1 cup, add enough water
ing to 1 cup. If more than 1 cup, boil
n.

---

1 cup soy sauce
¼ cup sake
1 large clove garlic, crushed
1 dried red pepper, crushed
2 tablespoons fresh ginger root, grated

Combine all ingredients.

To marinate insects, place them in the sauce
for several hours, or if in a hurry, simmer for
20 minutes and cool.

Garlic Butter Fried Insects

¼ cup butter
6 cloves garlic, crushed
1 cup cleaned insects*

Melt butter in fry pan. Reduce heat. Sauté
garlic in butter for 5 minutes. Add insects.
Continue sautéeing for 10-15 minutes,
stirring occasionally.

*Mealworms are especially delicious prepared
in this manner.

THE SEXUAL POLITICS OF MEAT

Carol Adams

Continuum, 1990

Feminist-vegetarian critical theory.

THE AESTHETICS OF
THE JAPANESE LUNCHBOX

Kenji Ekuan

MIT Press, 2000

The lunchbox
as a key to
understanding
Japanese
civilization.

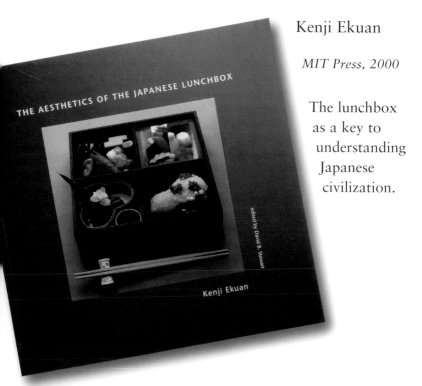

Tenth Anniversary Edition

The
Sexual
Politics
of Meat

*A Feminist-Vegetarian
Critical Theory*

Carol J. Adams

BOMBPROOF YOUR HORSE

Sgt Rick Pelicano

J.A. Allen, 2004

How to desensitize your horse to loud noises.

Bombproof Your Horse

Teach Your Horse to Be Confident, Obedient, and Safe No Matter What You Encounter

SGT. RICK PELICANO
with LAUREN TJADEN

COYOTES I HAVE KNOWN

John Duncklee

University of Arizona Press, 1996

Memoir.

COYOTES
I HAVE KNOWN

JOHN DUNCKLEE

277 SECRETS YOUR SNAKE WANTS YOU TO KNOW

Paulette Cooper

Ten Speed Press, 1999

Manual for owners of snakes.

RATS FOR THOSE WHO CARE

Dennis Kelsey-Wood

TFH Publications, 1995

Manual for owners of rats.

277 SECRETS
Your SNAKE ˄ Lizard
and

WANTS YOU TO KNOW

Unusual and Useful Information
for Snake Owners & Snake Lovers

PAULETTE COOPER

THE CARE AND FEEDING OF STUFFED ANIMALS

Glen Knape

Harry N. Abrams, 1983

Manual for owners of stuffed animals.

The Care and Feeding of
Stuffed Animals

By Glen Knape

KNITTING WITH DOG HAIR

Kendall Crolius

St Martin's Griffin, 1994

Craft projects.

*Trevor loves the dog sweater made by
his grandmother, Patricia Crolius.*

"For those who dread being in fashion's doghouse, there is hope—in the form of an all-natural fiber that can help you put on the dog." —*People* magazine

Knitting

WITH

Dog Hair

Better a sweater from a dog you know and love than from a sheep you'll never meet

Stop VACUUMING and START KNITTING!

KENDALL CROLIUS *and* ANNE MONTGOMERY

KNITTING IN THE FAST LANE

Christina L. Holmes & Mary Colucci

Krause Publications, 2001

Craft projects.

Knitting
in the
Fast Lane

▸▸▸ More than 35 projects for all skill levels

Christina L. Holmes
and Mary Colucci

TEA BAG FOLDING

Tiny Van Der Plas & Janet Wilson

Search Press, 2001

Craft projects.

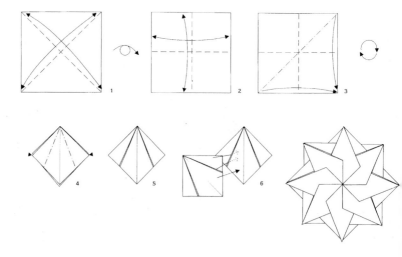

TEA BAG
FOLDING

Tiny Van Der Plas & Janet Wilson

SEARCH PRESS

TOOTHPICK SCULPTURE & ICE-CREAM STICK ART

Bruce Bowman

Sterling, 1976

Craft projects.

*Built entirely of ice-cream sticks,
this giant Eiffel Tower model is shown
with its creator Keith Goodlander.*

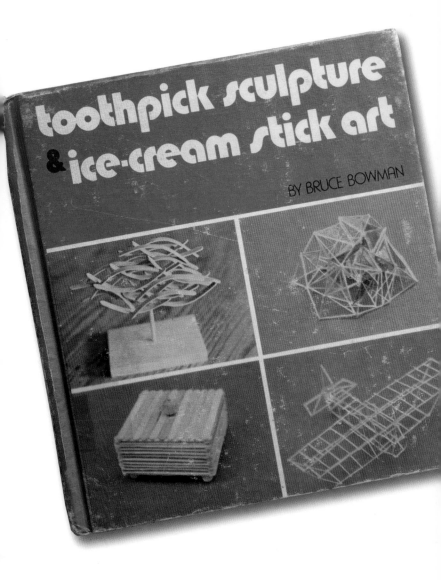

toothpick sculpture & ice-cream stick art

& ice-cream stick art

BY BRUCE BOWMAN

DO-IT-YOURSELF BRAIN SURGERY
& Other Home Skills

Stewart Cowley

Frederick Muller, 1981

Fun projects to try at home.

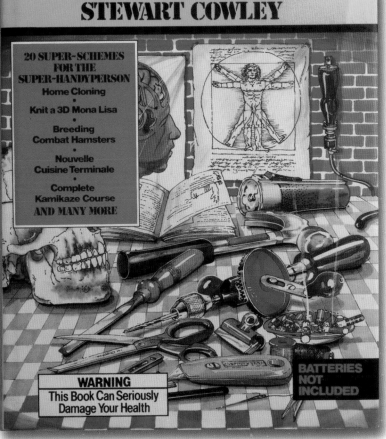

WOOD CARVING WITH A CHAINSAW

Lyn Mangan

Kangaroo Press, 1997

Craft projects.

WARNING

The instructions in this book are no substitute for proper training. Chainsaw carving should **not** be attempted by inexperienced chainsaw handlers. Seek professional advice **first**. Training courses are available—see footnote on p. 10.

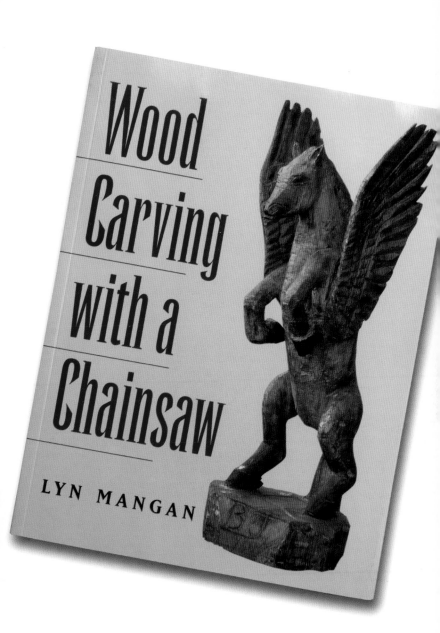

Wood Carving with a Chainsaw

LYN MANGAN

REUSING OLD GRAVES

Douglas Davies & Alastair Shaw

Shaw & Sons, 1994

Research into public opinion on the subject.

Soul passes on and Trust in God	54
Soul passes on and Reincarnation	26
Soul passes on and Resurrection	21
Resurrection and Trust in God	11
End of Life and Reincarnation	8

Table 8.10: Choice of Two Afterlife Beliefs.

REUSING OLD GRAVES

A Report on Popular British Attitudes

by

Douglas Davies

and

Alastair Shaw

 Shaw & Sons

FANCY COFFINS TO MAKE YOURSELF

Dale Power

Schiffer, 2001

Craft projects.

Fancy Coffins

To Make Yourself

Dale Power

A Schiffer Book for Woodworkers

IF YOU WANT CLOSURE IN YOUR RELATIONSHIP,
Start with Your Legs

Big Boom

Fireside, 2007

Dating advice.

A GUIDE TO
UNDERSTANDING
MEN
If You
Want Closure
in Your
Relationship,
Start with
Your Legs

BIG
BOOM

PEOPLE WHO DON'T KNOW THEY'RE DEAD
How They Attach Themselves to Unsuspecting Bystanders and What to Do About It

Gary Leon Hill

Weiser, 2005

How to handle unwanted attention from the spirit world.

People Who Don't
Know They're Dead

GARY LEON HILL

I WAS TORTURED BY THE PYGMY LOVE QUEEN

Jasper McCutcheon

Nazca Plains Corporation, 2007

Erotic novel.

GOD MAKES SEX GREAT!

Dr Renier Holtzhausen & Professor Hennie Stander

Metropolis Ink, 2001

Self-help manual for Christians.

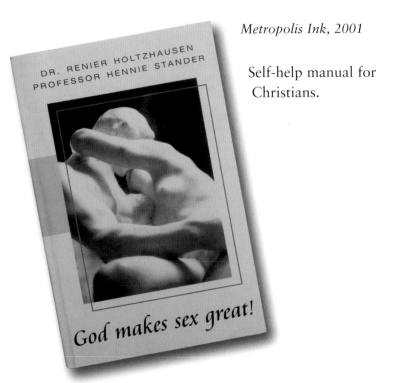

I Was Tortured By
the Pygmy Love Queen

Jasper McCutcheon

CELTIC SEX MAGIC
For Couples, Groups, and Solitary Practitioners

Jon G. Hughes

Destiny Books, 2001

How to practise Celtic sex rituals.

CELTIC

FOR COUPLES, GROUPS, &

SEX

SOLITARY PRACTITIONERS

MAGIC

JON G. HUGHES

THE BIG BOOK OF LESBIAN HORSE STORIES

Alisa Surkis & Monica Nolan

Kensington, 2002

Collection of short stories.

THE LESBIAN S/M SAFETY MANUAL

Pat Califia

Lace Publications, 1988

Tips for practising safe sex.

The Big Book of Lesbian Horse Stories

FIRST SHOCKING PRINTING!

of Lesbian Horse Stories

When these Sapphic sisters saddle up, ecstasy is only a hoofbeat away!

By ALISA SURKIS
and MONICA NOLAN

A KENSINGTON BOOK

SIX-LEGGED SEX
The Erotic Lives of Bugs

James K. Wangberg

Fulcrum, 2001

The sexual behaviour of insects.

SIX-LEGGED SEX

The Erotic Lives of Bugs

JAMES K. WANGBERG

Illustrations by Marjorie C. Leggitt

CONFESSIONS OF A PAGAN NUN

Kate Horsley

Shambhala, 2001

Historical novel.

AFTER THE ORGY
Toward a Politics of Exhaustion

Dominic Pettman

State University of New York,
2002

Cultural theory.

confessions
of a
pagan nun

a novel

kate horsley

TATTOOED MOUNTAIN WOMEN AND SPOON BOXES OF DAGHESTAN

Robert Chenciner, Gabib Ismailov
& Magomedkhan Magomedkhanov

Bennett & Bloom, 2006

Illustrated record of a system of folk medicine.

TATTOOED MOUNTAIN WOMEN AND SPOON BOXES OF DAGHESTAN

Magic medicine symbols in silk, stone, wood and flesh

Robert Chenciner, Gabib Ismailov & Magomedkhan Magomedkhanov

READING TOES
Your Feet as Reflections of Your Personality

Imre Somogyi

C. W. Daniel Company, 1997

Natural-healing manual.

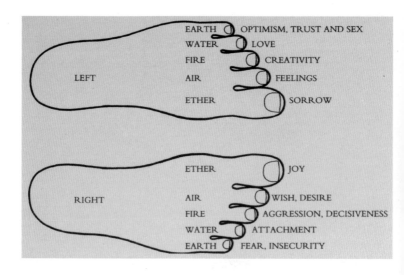

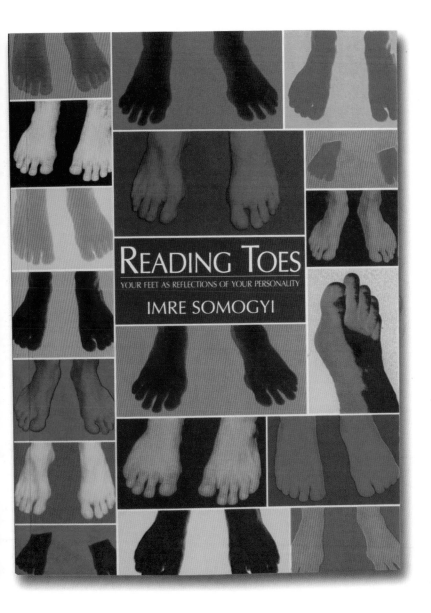

READING TOES
YOUR FEET AS REFLECTIONS OF YOUR PERSONALITY

IMRE SOMOGYI

NATURAL BUST ENLARGEMENT WITH TOTAL MIND POWER
How to Use the Other 90% of Your Mind to Increase the Size of Your Breasts

Donald L. Wilson MD

Total Mind Power Institute, 1979

Creative visualization techniques.

NATURAL BUST ENLARGEMENT WITH TOTAL MIND POWER

DONALD L. WILSON, M.D.

HOW TO USE
THE OTHER
90% OF YOUR MIND
TO INCREASE
THE SIZE OF
YOUR BREASTS

WHOSE BOTTOM?
A Lift-the-Flap Book

Moira Butterfield

Ladybird, 2000

Children's picture book.

ARCHAEOLOGY IN
THE AMERICAN BOTTOM

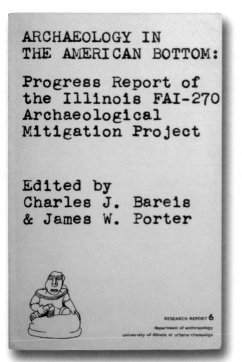

Charles J. Bareis
& James W. Porter
(editors)

University of Illinois, 1981

Archaeological project's
progress report.

Ladybird

1-3 years

Whose Bottom?

A lift-the-flap book

LIVING WITH CRAZY BUTTOCKS

Kaz Cooke

Penguin, 2001

Novel.

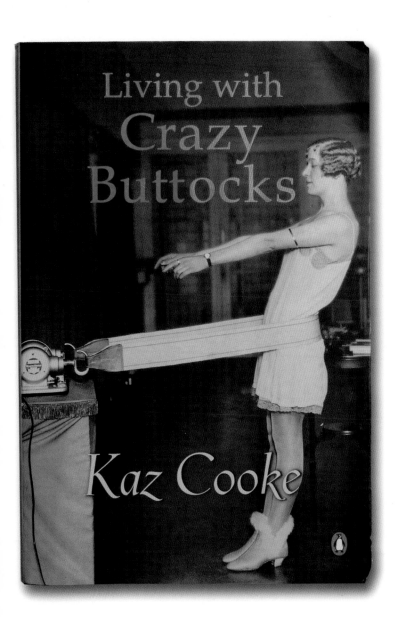

Living with
Crazy
Buttocks

Kaz Cooke

HOW TO SHIT IN THE WOODS
An Environmentally Sound Approach to a Lost Art

Kathleen Meyer

Ten Speed Press, 1989

Manual for fans of the great outdoors.

THE INTERNATIONAL BEST-SELLER WITH OVER 1 MILLION COPIES IN PRINT

2nd
Edition Revised

HOW TO SHIT IN THE WOODS

*An environmentally
sound approach
to a lost art*

Kathleen Meyer

OUTHOUSES OF ALASKA

Harry M. Walker

Epicenter Press, 1996

Illustrated coffee-table book.